T0395612

SAVE
he Trees

FIRST EDITION
Series Editor Penny Smith; **Art Editor** Leah Germann; **US Editors** Elizabeth Hester, John Sear
DTP Designer Almudena Díaz; **Pre-Production Producer** Nadine King; **Producer** Sara Hu;
Picture Research Myriam Megharbi; **Dinosaur Consultant** Dougal Dixon;
Reading Consultant Linda Gambrell, PhD

THIS EDITION
Editorial Management by Oriel Square
Produced for DK by WonderLab Group LLC
Jennifer Emmett, Erica Green, Kate Hale, *Founders*

Editors Grace Hill Smith, Libby Romero, Michaela Weglinski;
Photography Editors Kelley Miller, Annette Kiesow, Nicole DiMella;
Managing Editor Rachel Houghton; **Designers** Project Design Company;
Researcher Michelle Harris; **Copy Editor** Lori Merritt; **Indexer** Connie Binder; **Proofreader** Larry S
Reading Specialist Dr. Jennifer L. Albro; **Curriculum Specialist** Elaine Larson

Published in the United States by DK Publishing
1745 Broadway, 20th Floor, New York, NY 10019

Copyright © 2023 Dorling Kindersley Limited
DK, a Division of Penguin Random House LLC
23 24 25 26 10 9 8 7 6 5 4 3 2 1
001-333919-June/2023

A catalog record for this book
is available from the Library of Congress.
HC ISBN: 978-0-7440-7239-6
PB ISBN: 978-0-7440-7240-2

DK books are available at special discounts when purchased in bulk for sales promotions, premiums,
fundraising, or educational use. For details, contact: DK Publishing Special Markets,
1745 Broadway, 20th Floor, New York, NY 10019
SpecialSales@dk.com

Printed and bound in China

The publisher would like to thank the following for their kind permission to reproduce their images:
a=above; c=center; b=below; l=left; r=right; t=top; b/g=background

123RF.com: bmf2218 9bl, Leo Lintang 14br, Mihtiander 4-5cr, Christian Mueringer 9bc, Svetlana Yefimkina 9br;
Dreamstime.com: Monika Adamczyk 28bc, 31clb, Alekseyrezin 20bc, Andreistanescu 6-7, Andrew Astbury 13br,
Daseaford 24-25, Dfikar 22br, Dibrova 23br, Hywit Dimyadi 15bc, Max Dimyudl 14-15, Chanchai Duangdoosan 1cb,
Ecophoto 23bl, Elena Elisseeva 14bc, Filmfoto 3cb, 7bl, Nattapol Jaiinpol 19bl, Jmaca09 12br, Ying Feng Johansson 2
Tyler Keim 22-23, Kenmind76 10br, Sergii Kolesnyk / givaga 28br, Leonidikan 18-19, 31cla, Lovelyday12 26-27,
Nailotl Mendez 28-29, Ruud Morijn 20-21, 31cl, Nomadsoul1 4cl, Olgakotsareva 8br, Rangizzz 26br, Manfred Ruckszio
Smileus 18br, Sommai Sommai 6br, T.w. Van Urk 13bl, 31tl, Vladvitek 24br, Wacpan 29bc, James Wheeler 27br, Zerbor 2
Ziggymars 17bc, Zoom-zoom 12-13, Andrii Zorii 15br; **Getty Images / iStock:** amenic181 19bc, Camrocker 16bc,
Deyangeorgiev 11ca, drnadig 21bc, E+ / grandriver 16-17, Sieboldianus 10-11; **Shutterstock.com:** Manny DaCunha 16b
Purino 8-9, Inna Reznik 17bl, 31bl, Sirtravelalot 30

Cover images: *Front:* **Shutterstock.com:** BlueRingMedia bc, GraphicsRF.com bl, br, MuchMania b/g;
Back: **Dreamstime.com:** Vladimir Zadvinskii / Vldmr cr, tr; *Spine:* **Shutterstock.com:** BlueRingMedia

All other images © Dorling Kindersley
For more information see: www.dkimages.com

For the curious
www.dk.com

SAVE
he Trees

Ruth A. Musgrave

We need trees.
We need tall trees.

We need short trees. We need young and old trees.

young tree

old tree

Trees clean the air.
Their leaves
make shade.
Trees keep us cool
on a sunny day.

leaves

Trees give us food.
Lots of food.
Yum. Fruit or nuts?
Which do you like best?

fruit

nuts

Animals need trees.
They live in trees.
They find their food
in trees.
They raise their babies
in the branches.

branches

Wood comes from trees.
We use wood to build our homes.

wood

Trees make us happy.
Lean on a trunk to rest
and enjoy the day.
We cannot live
without trees.

trunk

What do trees need?
Trees need sunlight.
They need a lot of
room to grow.

sunlight

Trees need clean water.
Their roots
take in water.
The roots share it with
the rest of the tree.

roots

Trees need clean air. It helps them grow big and strong.

big trees

Trees also need our help. Sometimes we cut down too many trees. That means fewer trees.

cutting trees

You can help save trees.
You save trees when you use less paper.
You save trees when you recycle.
Do things that help keep the water clean.

recycle

You can plant seeds
to grow more trees.
You can learn
about trees.
Tell others about
them, too.

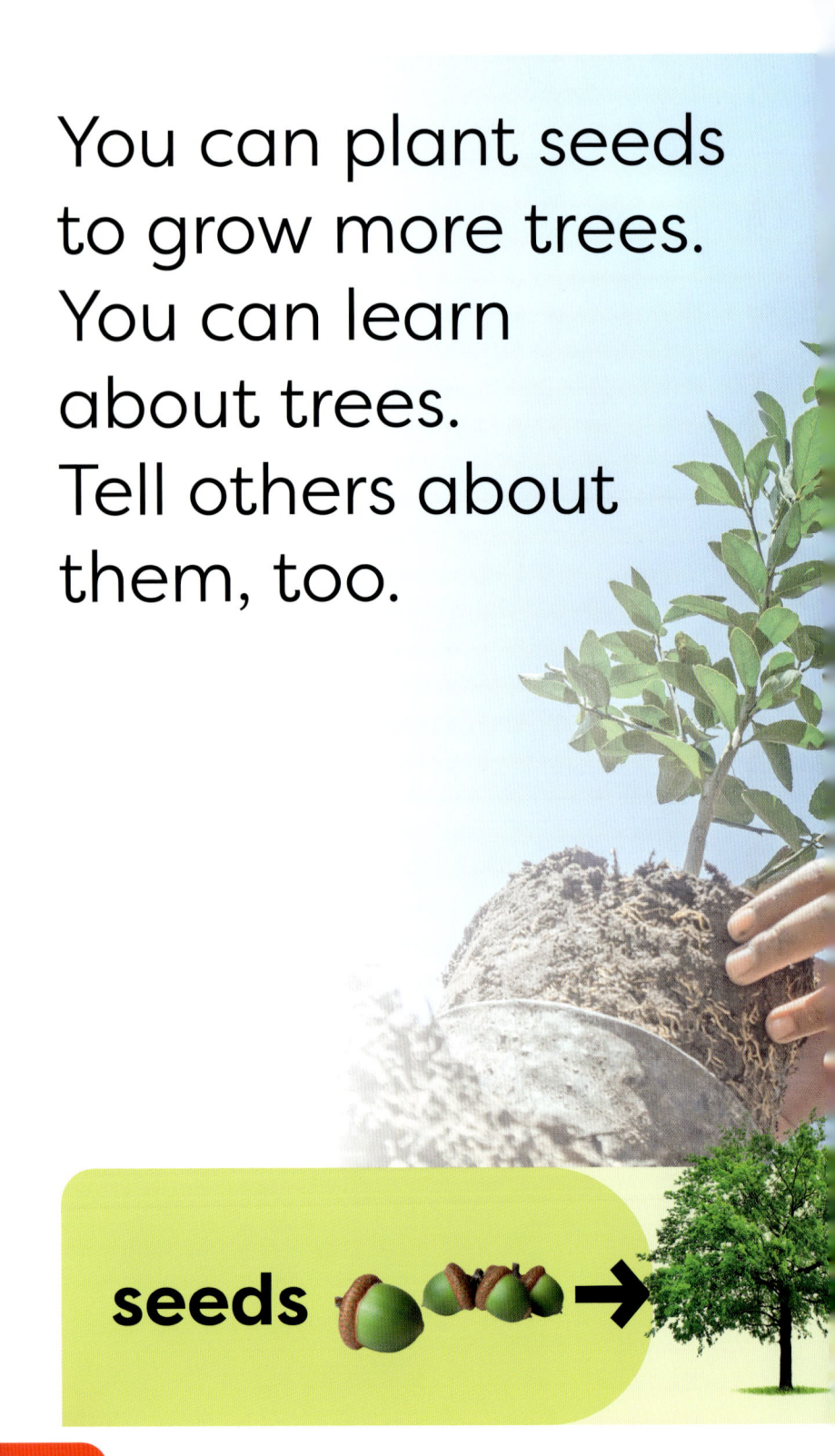

seeds

Hug a tree.
Love a tree.
Take care of trees.

Glossary

branches
the parts of a tree that grow out from the trunk

leaves
the parts of a plant that take in sunlight to help a plant grow

root
a part of a tree that holds a tree in the ground and takes in water

seed
a part of a plant that grows into a new plant

trunk
the main part of a tree that grows up from the roots

Quiz

Answer the questions to see what you have learned. Check your answers with an adult.

1. How do trees help the air?

2. Name three things trees need.

3. True or False: Animals raise their babies in trees.

4. What kinds of food do trees give us?

5. How can you grow more trees?

1. Trees clean the air 2. Sunlight, room to grow, and clean water
3. True 4. Fruit and nuts 5. Plant seeds